STICKMAKING TALES

LEO GOWAN

WITH DRAWINGS BY FRANK DAY

COCH-Y-BONDDU BOOKS

Author's dedication.

My thanks to the many who contributed - even unwittingly - over the years, to the making of this book. In particular I would like to thank Eileen Dye who typed the manuscript and Frank Day who contributed the illustrations.

First edition July 1996.
Published by Coch-y-bonddu Books, Machynlleth.

ISBN 0 9528510 0 8

Published & distributed by
COCH-Y-BONDDU BOOKS
MACHYNLLETH, POWYS, SY20 8DJ
Tel 01654 702837 Fax 01654 702857

Printed and bound in Great Britain by
Biddles Ltd, Guildford and King's Lynn

1
A Night To Remember

I'm often asked where I get my deer antler. Here's where I got my first.

I was just a lad and had to go into hospital to have my appendix seen to. The local Cottage Hospital stood in its own large grounds, only 100 yards from my home, down at the bottom of the street. I had mistaken the admission-time so while I waited I had a stroll around outside. Bequeathed by a rich local benefactor, the building had a thirty-yard-deep front-lawn, edged at the back by a shrubbery of large laurel bushes, with a strip of woodland beyond. I could just make out the roof of our house between the trees.

I stood goggle-eyed by the old stone coach-house, now used as an ambulance-bay, with its array of big-game horns, kudu, eland and buffalo, high up on the walls above the doors. But when I strolled over the lawn I saw something else that really took my eye. A magnificent pair of twelve-pointer red-deer antlers were artistically fixed by their frontal bone, eight feet up an old ash tree on a large round bole. Talk about the Monarch of the Glen. Did I not fancy them!

Following the operation I ended up in a ward overlooking the lawn. I was in the end bed and could just make out the antlers against the trunk with the trees in the background, and for the few days that I lay there my imagination ran riot. I had been to the Highlands hiking and camping two or three times and had glimpsed deer occasionally up on the tops, but all the antlers I had seen were still firmly attached to their owners. I had plenty of wood sticks of various sorts but those antlers, now... How I wished I could get my hands on them!

Ten days after being discharged from hospital my mind was made up. I slipped away down the street one night just after dark and climbed over the hospital fence. Away from the light of the last street lamp it was dark in the little wood, and even darker when I started crawling through the laurels, guided only by the lights of the hospital wards. Finally I came to the edge of the lawn. My sense of direction had been good, and just off to one side stood the old ash tree, the antlers only just visible at certain angles against the sky. I straightened up to move nearer to the tree and there was a loud crack as I stood on a dead branch. Came a shrill scream from the verandah in front of the ward, "Nurse! Nurse!" I twisted around and dropped back smartly to my knees and tunnelled along deeper into the bushes. More than a little scared, I turned and peered through the leaves back towards the building.

There was a bed at one end of the verandah and a nurse coming through the door behind! I could hear a quick gabble from the vague figure in the bed who was gesticulating in my direction. Ready to make a run for it, I could hear the soothing voice of the nurse, who left after a while, switching on the verandah light, which fortunately didn't illuminate as far as my hidey-hole. I waited. The figure in the bed was restless and I could see her peering at intervals across the lawn in my direction. However, after a long ten minutes or so she seemed to subside against the pillows, and I gave her another few minutes to settle down then crept back cautiously towards the tree. I was more than a little apprehensive - but still set on having those antlers.

There were nice big burrs at intervals up the back of the trunk, making it an easy climb, keeping the trunk between me and the hospital. I got up to six feet or so, then peeped around gingerly. All quiet from the verandah and there were the antlers just slightly overhead and within easy reach. I eased out the big screwdriver from my back pocket and pushed the blade between the skull-bone and the burr and levered with one hand whilst hanging on to one antler with the other.

A fixing-nail or screw screeched raucously and I clung there petrified as a crescendo of screams came from the verandah. More lights, doors opening, and three or four nurses this time. Finally the formidable figure of Matron, a large well-upholstered tyrant with a voice on her that could have drilled a Brigade of Guards. The near hysterical voice grated away and again pointed over in my direction. I scrambled a little further up the trunk, clung tight, and tried to pass off as an extra large ash burr. (Never mind laughing, you try it sometime). Torches were flashing alarmingly across the lawn and white-clad figures flitted to and fro as Matron gave her orders. One nurse came to the base of the tree, then - what a relief - turned back towards the building. I could hear reassuring voices from the verandah and eventually everyone trooped away and all was quiet again. My heart got back to normal, slowly, but this time the figure on the bed just *knew* that I was there. She stared my way intently for long periods, turned away, then would suddenly swing her head around, no doubt hoping to surprise the intruder.

I had lost the screwdriver in the kerfuffle and had to make up my mind quickly. I could get back down the tree and creep away, tail between my legs - or I could go for it. Having risked so much up to now I was not going to leave without one last effort.

Reaching slowly around I twisted and gripped an antler in each hand, a deep breath, and I stepped off the burr I had been perched on, swung my whole body around the trunk and let the antlers take my full weight. They pulled away from the trunk with a reverberating crack and I landed with a tremendous crash in the middle of a big laurel bush.

Piercing screams non-stop from the verandah, lights on all over, and voices raised as I floundered out of the bushes, keeping a tight grip on my prize. Then I was away through the trees with no attempt at stealth, over the fence, and scarpering up our street.

There was nothing in the local paper about a hospital intruder - but shortly afterwards a big alsatian-dog belonging to the gardener (hitherto little seen but reputed to have three rows of teeth) started roaming the grounds. He developed a nasty habit of snuffling at the fence when we were footballing in the street and I refused to play in goal at that end. I got a rollicking from my Da for losing his screwdriver, and my Ma wasn't too happy either at having to repair a big rip in the leg of my trousers.

I got to thinking afterwards - what would have happened if the antler hadn't broken away? I would have been dangling there like Tarzan on a bad day, except that he didn't trapeze around in the dark, and besides, neither did I have a leopard-skin jock-strap.

But I was happy ... I'd been on safari and I'd got my trophies. Now I *could* make antler handles.

2
The Grave Robbers

The enthusiastic stickmaker, forever acquisitive in obtaining the raw material of his craft, gets his horn by every means at his disposal - stolen; presented; captured; bought; won; given; taken; bartered; found; acquired by accident; bequeathed; bid for; fallen off the back of a lorry etc. But robbing a grave - "That's a bit off" I can hear you say...

I hadn't seen Jonty for about ten years when I bumped into him shortly after moving back to the village. I remembered that, not long before I had left the area, he had married a widow, a big domineering sort of woman, and this had caused a lot of gossip at the time. The general feeling seemed that she had talked him into it, and it was the accepted view that Jonty was a sandwich or two short of a picnic anyway. But she had a cottage of her own with an acre or two including two small meadows and an orchard, and Jonty had always lived with his parents in a two-up and two-down terraced house along with his brother and three sisters.

He had hardly changed at all. Still the black wellies, half turned down, (I never even knew that black wellies were still being made) and a well-worn navy donkey-jacket with a leatherette shoulder-patch bearing the name of some national civil-engineering firm. The corduroy trousers were so old that they no longer whistled when he walked; and they looked in fact as if they could have walked by themselves. He could never be described as a snappy dresser.

"What fettle, Jonty?" I asked.

"Canny, lad, very canny. How's yersel?"

We chewed the fat about the old days. (We had both attended the village school and grew up together, and we've passed a lot of water under the bridge since that time.)

"Still keep the hens, then, Jonty?"

"Why aye, thourty or fourty - gorra lot of chickens just noo - and a few geese and ducks. Stable a few ponies for them young lasses at the riding-school as weel. Muck's handy for the fruit-bushes."

"How about the goats, still got them?"

"Oh aye, fower nannies, three kids and a billy."

"Have you still got that big Billy then? Must be a canny age now, then."

"Naw, died last year, did owd Billy, eighteen year owd he wor; reet smelly bugger an' all. Gorra new young billy, noo, fower year owd."

I remembered "Owd Billy" alright, He had ruled the orchard and when helping Jonty picking apples the year I had left the village we had both been dunted by those horns a few times - HORNS!!!

"Had big horns, owd Billy, didn't he?" I asked casually.

"Big enough, lad. Must have been three foot, I reckon - used to scratch his arse, ye remember, by leaning his heid back."

"What did you do with him, then - knackers-yard?"

"Ne fear - the wife thowt the world of him, she did, I reckon his beard reminded her of Isaac, her first. Remember him? Smelly owd bugger he wor - nigh as bad as Billy. Buried in the orchard, anyroad. Billy that is, not Isaac. Incinerated *him*. Keeps him in a cigar box, atop of the mantelpiece."

He smiled. "Knocked him off the other week, by accident, like. Bugger scattered aal ower the hearth and the rug. Swept him up as best aa could but had to top him up wi' ash oot of the stove. Needed to shake the rug oot of the back door. Should hiv seen them hens come running. Good job the buggers aren't layin' at the minnit, fancy hevin' bits of thon bugger in your eggshell! Enuff to put ye off yer breakfast. Bloody good job *She* wasn't in either, at the time, aa might ha' ended up on the mantelpiece alongside him."

"Three feet long, you reckon; in the orchard?" says I, quite excited. "Give you ten quid for them."

Jonty looked a mite perplexed. "Ten pun? But aa telled ye, man, he's been deid this year gone. We canna bring him back noo."

"But the horns'll be alright, Jonty, they reckon they last for fifteen years in the ground." (I don't know where I had heard that rather esoteric snippet of information, but it had stuck in my mind).

"But aa couldn't dig him up, man, the wife would go doolally. Thowt a lot of him she did."

But I could see he was weakening. His wife controlled the purse strings in that household and kept Jonty short.

"But we needn't tell her, man, Jonty. Wait until she's out or something."

And that is just what we did. 'The Wife' was seen off on a bus trip - 'Mystery Tour to South Shields' - "gan every year" according to Jonty - and we hurried back to the orchard. Easy enough to see the site of the grave, the grass greener and more luxurious. We tied up the young billy first, to forestall him dunting us, then carefully cut around the head area and rolled back the turf. After a few scrapes with a trowel the tip of one of the horns came into view. There was an ant's nest next to the grave and skull was quite clean, apart from a matted pad of hair. The horns pulled away easily and were in good condition. Not three foot long but twenty-seven inches exactly. Billy had been piebald and the horn was variegated in colour; much nicer than if he had been black or grey, when the horn would have been black and not so attractive. One third towards the tip was solid and both would make good horn handles, after drying out for a while.

"Christmas cums early" said Jonty, pocketing the handful of smaller change he had asked for instead of a ten-pound note. "If she fund that" he said, "Aa *wud* end up on the mantelpiece!"

"Keep me the horns, mind, when this billy goes, Jonty."

"Hae nee feer, lad, they'll be off lang afore this one's buried. And give us a hand filling this hole in else *ye*'ll end up on wor mantelpiece, alongside me!"

3
The Art Of Carving

"Can you teach me how to carve?" said one of the evening-class.

"It's no use you asking me," I replied, "I can't carve."

"What about that badger of yours, then; and that duck? They're carvings, aren't they!"

Actually (although I admit to a little bias) I thought that both badger and duck were quite reasonable; not show-winners admittedly but maybe *class*-winners. Depending on the opposition naturally. But in my mind I had not carved them; both are not difficult subjects to shape up and that is just what I had done. I wouldn't attempt a fox or collie, for instance, as both are notoriously difficult to do well. The fact is of course that there is nothing mystical about being a carver, who is indubitably an artist. You must have it initially, otherwise you are but an artisan; a skilled craftsman without a doubt, but the artist has that something extra which sets him apart.

The author of the book on "creative woodcarving" who claims that "anyone who has reasonable co-ordination, bodily control, strength and eyesight can learn to carve" is of course justified in trying to promote sales of his book. But he is talking virtual nonsense. I should like to think that I could satisfy the criteria quoted, and in addition I still have most of my own teeth, and a good part of my hair. I have been carrying a stick since about the time when I learned to read without moving my lips, and have made sticks for the greater part of that period - but I can't carve a fancy stick. I have books on carving, too, and I can use hand- and power-tools, neither am I easily discouraged by failure - but I can't carve fancy sticks.

If I had to describe a carver, I should define him as someone who can present a reasonably accurate and lifelike representation of the required subject in the medium used, whether wood, horn, antler or whatever. Unfortunately many of the carvings seen in the stick world would not meet this criteria. We have all seen them - the collies with more than a passing resemblance to Gloucester Old Spots; the fox that can double for corgi or alsatian; the trout that could be any species from kipper to carp, and the pheasants that resemble eagles with rouged cheeks. These I would term bodge-ups, and if this seems unkind, just compare such crudities to others by artists where the subject is immediately identifiable and virtually *alive.* The creative carver can take a block of wood or other medium and see the subject in it before starting. Often, after even just a few minutes work, the basic shape is showing up.

Then there is the other, more common type of carver who can only copy. Given a pheasant head or a trout from the freezer; or more commonly, an illustration from a book, he can turn out a reasonable replica by dint of hard work, measuring with callipers, etc. *But* the essential life-like look is usually absent in the finished product. These could be termed the second-eleven artists. The problem with using illustrations is in seeing the work in two dimensions only. As a result the carving is often foreshortened or even distorted through lack of depth perception. The best carvers do not have this problem, and have also the ability to scale up or down in proportion, this being considerably more difficult than it sounds. You will often see a stick with a blue-tit, a nuthatch or a woodpecker, life size and completely upsetting the balance and symmetry of a crook handle. Rarely will these birds be shown in miniature where they would look far more realistic on the stick. Carving in the smaller format is naturally much more difficult than in life-size!

Far be it from me to discourage any would be carvers from trying their hands, but it *is* a gift, and you'll never *learn* it if you don't have it in the first instance. But don't be discouraged; at least ninety-nine per cent of stickmakers haven't got it either!

4
Lucky

I was staying the weekend with my cousin, and he took me to the village show on the Saturday. I could have been at our own village show, they were so similar. You won't meet with the like nowadays. All roads led to the show-field and the village must have been virtually deserted by mid-morning. You paid your money at the gate, and held out your hand to be stamped on the wrist. The ink was invariably purple and you always worried about it rubbing off. It never did, but if it had you would have to pay again to re-enter the ground.

The local brass band was oompah-ing away noisily, not quite in tune; they seemed to have three or four uniforms between the dozen of them. Donkey-rides, very popular at thrupence a go; a catapult range for the dads and lads - First-prize a cocoa-tin of suitable sized ball-bearings, a Tug-o-war, of course, between rival pub teams, and naturally a "Bonny Baby" competition. I doubt if the Judge had volunteered for this one, but it could have been worse I suppose - what if it had been a "Plain Baby" contest! You could more than likely pick the winner of that one easily enough, but the mother would probably be larger than the Judge, and with a gob on her that would shift the wax out of your ears. Mind you, I doubt if there would be many entries and if he had any gumption a dead-heat would be safest. Another tricky one was the class for "The Dog With The Prettiest Owner". Apart from picking the winner on looks, it was fairly obvious that a good number of dogs had been "borrowed" for the occasion. But I liked the one for "The Dog That Looks Most Like His Master" (or perhaps it was the other way round). This was won by an elderly grizzled Lakeland terrier with an even more grizzled owner. Obviously both from the same litter.

We gorged on fizzy lemonade and ice-cream cornets, which lay a mite uneasily with our egg sandwiches. My cousin left me to visit the zebra-striped 'Flower Show and Garden Produce' marquee to see how his Da had fared with his '6 Different Veg'. entry, and I headed for the other 'Kitchen and Handicrafts.' All trestle-tables swathed in fine lace and needlework, cakes and jams, pickle and chutneys, home-made wine and art. I made my way towards the woodwork section; model houses, boats, gipsy-caravans and marquetry, poker-work and - right in the corner - sticks! Just a tiddly little display really with perhaps twentyfive or thirty entries. The expected wood thumbsticks, two or three root-ash and a knobbly old blackthorn. Also a five-foot hazel shank complete with badges from places visited by the owner - Fort William, Oban, Skye, the Trossachs, - he obviously liked Scotland. There was a roe-antler thumbstick, and a riding crop handle with silver collar mounted on a thin hazel, and one horn-heid, a tup-horn market-stick. This had the red card for winner, (ten-bob prize-money), and I had a good look at it on the bench.

The shank was bent and the handle badly jointed, with a thick glue-line showing. It was varnished thickly from tip to toe and this had run in places, including one blob down the nose. The white was showing through both on the neck and the nose and one or two cracks here and there had been filled with bodge with a poor colour-match. The nose drooped and was below the level of the joint; also it was out of line with the neck. And it was rat-tailed. It would have been an ideal demonstration model in showing novices how *not* to make a horn-heid. Overall it was so rough that it would automatically qualify for the Badger's Bum Award at any stick-show. It had been perpetrated, not crafted.

I happened to overhear the maker modestly telling one of the Show committee that nobody had shown him how to work horn, and that he had "picked up all his skills" himself. Entirely self-taught, and a great admirer of the teacher, quite obviously. But the luck of it all, winning with such a stick!

Later we were strolling back through the village and saw the little postcard advert in the paper shop window:-

LUCKY

***LOST DOG**. Three legs; blind in left eye; large scar on throat. Left-ear torn - right-ear missing. Tail broken in two places - droops. Nails gone from right foreleg- limps a little. Bald, mangy patches on coat; scratches a lot. Several teeth broken. Recently castrated. Answers to the name of "Lucky".*

Probably belonged to the owner of the winning stick!

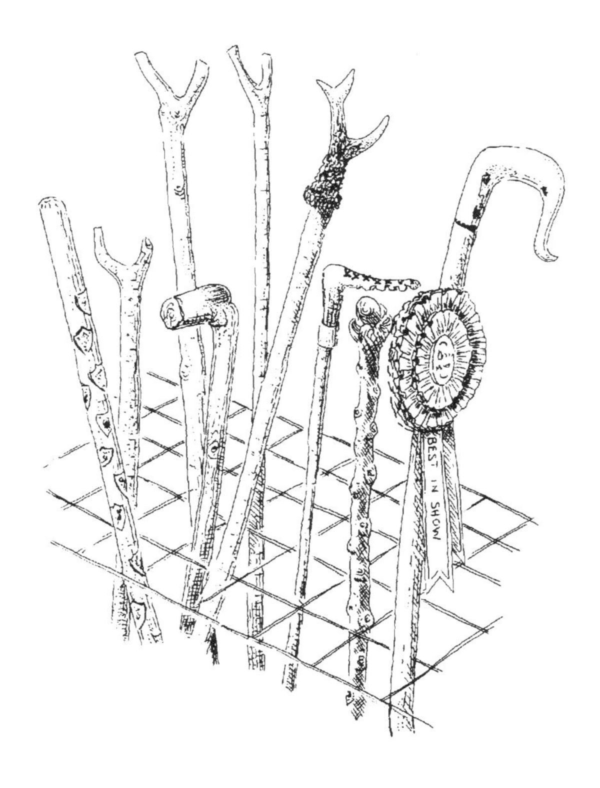

5
The Blackthorn

Arty always admitted to being a hearty eater, and at a height of 5 ft. 5 ins. and weighing fifteen-stone, who could doubt him. The only child of a widowed mother who doted on him, he often said that he could eat "two more taties than a pig". His weight definitely came from the plate.

I met him one day near the end of February, not long after I had finished stick-cutting for the season.

"Just the lad I wanted to see," he says. "Give us a hand - got me eye on a blackthorn."

The thicket had spread out from a hedge into the corner of the field, dense and seemingly impenetrable and twenty feet. or more deep. The stick he fancied was right in the middle with only the top two foot. or so in view.

"Bloody rabbit would be pushed to get in there, man, Arty. Place is nowt but a jungle."

"*Aa* will, though! Got me pruning saw, wi' a new blade. Had me eye on this'n for a bit." And he got down on his knees and started sawing at the base of the nearest bush. Job done, I helped him to drag the bush clear, then he wriggled into the gap and started again. I couldn't help him much this time as the opening was too narrow, but with a bit of heaving and cursing he managed to pull it out.

"Bugger that for a game of sojers," he says, "aa'm just cutting branches off from noo on, an' aa'll squeeze in best I can." He seemed to be managing alright for a few feet or so, until all I could see of him was his wellies and a hefty corduroyed backside sticking out of a particularly thick patch, when he lets out a yell,

"Aa'm stuck. Canna move!"

"Hang on," says I, "See if we can pull you oot."

"Ye'll bloody not, there's thorns digging in."

"Warraboot the saw, then, Arty, can you pass it oot?"

"Canna move me arm, man. Bloody thorns!"

"Hang on then. Have to get *my* saw. Be back as soon as I can."

It was at least two miles back home, mostly uphill, and it must have been about an hour and a half before I got back.

No sign of Arty, but there was a swathe of cut and flattened bushes completely through the thicket. A cart-horse couldn't have done better. There was no reply when I called at his home, but next morning when I went around there was a five-foot blackthorn shank propped up against the coal-house wall in the back-yard. Arty was by the fireside, sitting on the edge of his armchair, mother fussing around like a bumbler in a strange netty. He was getting stuck in at a pile of bacon-sandwiches on a dinner-plate. One ear looked a bit chewed, there was a long inflamed scratch on his neck, and both arms were bandaged from wrist to forearm.

"Got your stick, Arty, anyroad. Looks a real belter."

"'Tis that, lad. Bit of a struggle, mind, gettin' it."

"Howd'ye manage to get out of the bush, then? Ye wor weel stuck when aa left."

"Got me arm loose; up on me feet wi' a struggle, cut me stick, an' just cut 'n' pushed me way oot. Couldn' back up at aal - couldn' turn roond! Mind ye, one cheek wasn't half givin' me some stick aal the way back. Swelled reet up it wor by time aa got in. Sore wasn't innit. Had ti gan ti hospital. Norse gorrit oot. Bloody thorn, shudha' seen the bugger. Nigh on an inch long it wor. Gorra injection as weel, anti-titanius, like. Bloody needle like a poker. Ye wudha' thowt she'd ha' put it in me arm, like, but naw, had ti be me arse, didn' it? And in t'*other* cheek, as weel! Both buggers swelled up noo...

Bloody good stick, though, eh?"

6
Sod's Law

Sod's Law is around most of the time. I suppose that a rough definition would be that anything that can possibly go wrong - will go wrong, usually when least expected. And, to coin a phrase, more than likely there's sod-all that you can do to prevent that happening!

The simplest example in everyday life would be a typical morning rushing out to work. You've more than likely cut yourself shaving; the toast was burnt and that slice that you scraped down slipped and fell, landing marmalade-side-down. One of your shoelaces snapped, and when you finally got on the road, out of four traffic-lights, three were on red. Naturally you had forgotten your bait...

And what applies in every day life carries over of course to stickmaking; and not just in the workshop, either. I've ripped the backside or leg of a good pair of cords or moleskins several times when climbing over the fence into a wood or field. And if I trip over a bramble or branch, the hand flung out to ease the fall lands in some thistles or nettles. This could be put down to me being just a downright clumsy bugger. But even if I wasn't, you could almost bank on one of the wire staples giving way or a fence-rail breaking. The net result would be the same.

Sometimes other living creatures take a hand. I had just gone a short way across a field once, when I saw in the far corner a massive Hereford bull, backside up against that blackthorn thicket that I'd had my eye on for a year or two. He wasn't exactly snorting and pawing the ground, but looked as if he was just ticking over in neutral, all ready to slip into first for a flying start. Not that I gave him time to decide, but turned round smartly and ran for it. Slap into the middle of a massive bull-pat, must have been eighteen inches across. Fresh too. I was splattered up way past my knees. *And* I'd just polished my boots the night before. There was enough manure to scrape off my strides to start a new compost-heap in the garden. And when I looked back after scrambling out of the field, the bugger was still there in the same corner. He hadn't moved an inch. I never did get to look at those blackthorn as he was in the field for the next few months, and that was his favourite corner.

Then there was the time I pushed my way into a hazel-thicket along the lonnen, a likely looking place for shanks. Seconds later I came bursting out of the bush and ran back down the lonnen, arms waving around my head like a demented tick-tack man at the races. I had put a foot right into the middle of a wasps' nest, and ended up with a couple of dozen or so stings. And I never managed to look at those hazels either, nor have I ever risked going back. And that was twenty years ago.

When you are working with tools Sod's Law often involves your thumb. You know the sort of thing that happens; you're bashing away quite happily when the left thumb loses concentration and decides to go walkabout and ends up inevitably on the receiving end of the hammer. I remember vividly (how could I forget?) when I was pouring molten-lead into the drilled-out end of a wading-pole. This was blackthorn and the lead forced out the base of the thorn - which runs back into the centre of the wood - and molten lead ran down my thumb. The sort of happening that tests your patience a bit.

And when you are using a chisel or gouge which slips it's usually the thumb on the receiving end. The thumb can be repaired of course, given time, but it's a different matter if you're left with a nasty deep gouge in a nice piece of wood or horn... Also, try to prevent your thumb from remaining in the vice jaws when you are tightening them up to flatten a piece of horn.

Sometimes the right-hand doesn't know what the left thumb is up to. And if your workshop or shed is based on the deep-litter system, then it is obvious that Sod's Law will be lying in wait.

Sod's Law really comes into its own in horn-work. As a rule it doesn't show itself at first, but puts in an appearance after you've spent a fair bit of time and effort on the horn-heid. It's just shaping up nicely when that wrinkle develops into a crack...

Or the white comes to the surface just at a spot where it will catch the eye. Worst of the lot, and quite common too, is the blood clot. This is usually discovered late in the day, when you are just shaping up the nose of the crook after several hours hard work. If it's not too bad it might just discolour the horn, but at its worst it will have rotted, and you won't even be able to shape the nose. And horn often takes on a life of its own when under pressure in the vice. I've been dunted several times by pieces leaping out of the vice, and on one occasion had to retrieve a piece from the garden after it had gone through a window.

It's some slight consolation to know that Sod's Law works in *your* favour on occasion, when it has applied to someone else, that is. I've found over the years in the woods two or three knives, and once a short axe, all obviously belonging to stick-cutters. Several times I've come across a block-stick, usually draped over a branch and meant to be picked up later, and once I found a neat bundle of shanks propped up against a tree. And nobody around on these occasions. Makes up for the times when I've mislaid similar items, I suppose.

It's known as Murphy's Law in Ireland but no special name as far as I know applies in Wales and Scotland.

7
A Real Brahma

Seppy only made wood-sticks, and as he worked on a farm bordering on a well-wooded estate, he could always get plenty of shanks and block-sticks around the fields and the edges of the woods. He usually gave me the roe-antler that he came across occasionally, and also odd cow-horn from time to time (this being at a time when cows came complete with horns - and were allowed to wear them), so when he came round early that Sunday morning in November I could hardly refuse him.

"Got me eye on a belter of a stick," he says, "Give us a hand to get him. It's a real brahma!" So off we went, Seppy clutching an old bushman's saw. (Must be a block-stick, then, I reckoned.)

"Where is it, then, Sep?" I asked, as we left the village and cut over the fields.

"In the Dene," he says, "Hev to keep an eye oot for Owld Woody." The Dene was at one end of the estate, a mile or so from the village, and Woody, the gamekeeper, had chased us now and again as we roamed around the countryside. I knew my way around the estate roughly, as I had helped out as a beater occasionally when there was a pheasant shoot. Seppy, I fancy, knew it rather better, as he had lifted quite a few rabbits and pheasants there in his poaching jaunts since he started work.

"Ye havn't got your gun with ye, now have ye, Sep?" says I.

"Nee fear, lad, it's business the day."

It was an ash tree in the middle of the Dene, by the side of a narrow ride which ran the length of the wood. The stick was growing vertically up from a horizontal branch about ten or twelve feet up, and perhaps five to six feet along from the trunk. And it did look a belter, growing straight with no kinks. A real brahma, in fact. Seppy was a poor tree-climber, which is why he had asked me along, of course.

"Give us a push onto that first branch, then, Sep, then I'll manage." Once I was up on to this branch six-foot up, I shinned up a few feet, shuffled around the trunk half way and pulled myself up onto the branch I wanted. Two minutes to get my breath back, then with back to the trunk and legs straddling the branch, I shuffled cautiously along towards the stick.

"Hoy up the saw, Sep, an' try an' keep the handle reet way up." Easier said than done - on the first two attempts I nearly grabbed the blade, and the third time the blade went straight through my trousers and into my calf. "Bloody Hell! Sep, man, gan canny, else ye'll hev me off." Eventually, without further bloodshed, I managed to grab it, although I nearly fell off the branch as I reached out for it.

After a quick weighing up, I undercut the branch an inch behind where the stick grew, then undercut again six inches towards me. Then quickly I sawed off the part of the branch beyond the stick. The sawn part bounced off a lower branch, making quite a clatter on the way down.

"Hev to mek less noise, Sep, else Woody'll hear us."

"Naw," says he, "Sunday morn, reckon he'll be hevvin' a lie in the day."

He'd no sooner spoke than there was a loud shotgun blast no more than a hundred-yards away down the ride, followed by the pitter-patter of pellets through the trees a little nearer.

"Buggerit!" says Seppy in a loud whisper. "Bloody Woody! What's got him up? Keep ahaad, Tarzan, aa'll be back." And he grabbed the sawn-off branch, pulled it into some bushes to one side and scarpered away through the trees parallel to the ride, with me stuck up there like a shag on a rock. I had enough sense to shuffle backwards until my back met the trunk, then drew up my knees, partly to balance more easily, but mainly to hide my face. The saw I had looped over the little stump left beyond the stick, and it had hardly stopped swaying to-and-fro when I saw Woody a few yards away down the ride. He was glancing from side to side as he always did, no doubt looking for rabbit-fur or pheasant-feathers or other signs of poaching. He came straight up towards the tree and I was sure that he must see me. Then he stopped just underneath me. If he didn't see me he must surely see the saw! He knew something was not quite right, sure enough, but just didn't know what it was. He would look up at any time - but just then there was a another shot, way off down the ride.

Woody set off smartly in that direction, and I let my breath out. That bugger Sep must have had his gun with him after all! A couple of minutes later there was another bang further away again and off to one side. I sat there trying to puzzle out what was going on when a minute or two later Seppy gets back, coming from the direction of the last shot. "Saw it off, man," he gasps breathlessly, "and let's get oot of here." I did, then throwing down the saw I scrambled down. Seppy by then had sawn off the stick at about four-foot, and as it wasn't the occasion for tiptoeing through the tulips, we crashed through the bushes and trees, and were out of the Dene and over a field. There was a roar behind us and I looked back and there was Woody at the edge of the wood shaking his gun at us. He shouted something that I couldn't quite hear properly but ending in ... "Little Buggers!" We didn't stop of course, not until we'd covered another field, then flopped down behind a holly-bush to get our wind back.

"Thowt ye didn't hev your gun with ye, Sep," I said; quite narked.

"Didn't," he says, still winded.

"Then who was shooting, then?"

"Wasn't a gun, man. I had two bangers left over from Guy Fawkes last week. Kept them specially, just in case. Thowt they might come in handy the day, mebbe. Set one off, then run t'other side of wood, then set other'un off. Then run roond again and back to you. Aa'm fair knackered, man. And worraboot Woody, man? Bet he thowt he was being invaded!"

"*Ye*'re fair knackered!" I was highly indignant. "Worraboot me up the tree, then? Woody was reet underneath, man. Divvent ask me to help ye again, man. Buggerit, put years on me the day, ye have!"

"Got something for ye, anyroad," he says, pulling a nice rabbit out of a pocket. "Oot of one of me hangs set around the wood. Should ha' seen yersel', man, sitting up that tree there like a bloody big constipated owl. Worraboot me stick, anyway? Tellt ye it were a real brahma, noo, isn't it?" And it was.

The rabbit wasn't bad, either.

I got back to the village after twenty years away and bumped into Seppy not long afterwards. He was carrying a nicely oiled and well-kept ash market-stick. "Reckernise it?" he says. And it had certainly turned out well, and obviously been cherished.

"Was hoping to bump into ye. Heard ye was back. Got me eye on another one. Better nor this'n. Hoo aboot givvin' us a hand? - It's a real brahma!"

8
It's An Ill Wind

He never did like driving in the dark. The headlamps were pretty feeble and the heater likewise, with the windscreen misting up frequently. And those Morris Minor wipers, leaving a good part of the centre of the windscreen dirty. Wished he had set off earlier. Although he had directions how to get to his friend's cottage, he hadn't reckoned on this narrow winding country road, hemmed in on either side with earth banks topped by hawthorn hedge. It was starting to drizzle and leaves were swirling around in the wind. He switched on the wipers once again, dipped the headlamps and changed down to third for yet another blind bend. For a split second he glimpsed a small brown figure at his side of the road, followed by a jarring thud. The car stalled.

Heart racing and dreading what he would find (child? old woman?) he got out to investigate. The body lay sprawled a foot or so in front of the car, one headlamp reflecting broken glass from the other smashed one. There was tremendous relief when he realised that it wasn't human but a fair-sized animal, neck at a funny angle and presumably dead. Mind racing and wondering what on earth to do, he was bending gingerly over it, but stood up rather guiltily as the motor-bike came over the brow of the hill. It pulled up a few yards away.

"Trouble, lad?"

"I couldn't stop in time," he blurted out; "Just appeared in front of me. On the bend. Braked, but skidded a bit on the leaves."

"Let's hev a glim, then. See what's what." Brief examination... "Roe deer; deid aalreet. Brokken neck. Nivvor knew what hit it. Poor bugger!"

"Wasn't my fault. Didn't have time to brake properly. I'm sure it just jumped out that instant. Couldn't even swerve in time." He was nearly babbling.

"Thing is, lad, deer's game; and it's after dark. That's poachin', like, they reckon. Oot of season, as weel. Reet load of trubble, aa reckon ye're in."

Visions of his wife... ("They'll take you to court!; Name in the papers, as well!!; What'll me mother say?") "What can I do, then?" he said, desperation in his voice.

"Aa were you, lad; in your shoes, like, aa'd tell the Poliss. Be on the safe side, like. One in th' village; half mile up road. Forst hoose on left. Be best, aa reckon. Keep ye'sel reet. Gerraway there noo. Aa'll keep an eye on things here, like..."

Relief in his voice. "Sure you don't mind, then? I'll go now, be as quick as I can. Thanks!"

Ten minutes later he was back with the policeman, who was rather irate at being dragged away from his fireside. Doubtful at first if this was the scene of the accident; but yes, there were a few pieces of headlamp glass, and a chromed rim. But no deer - and no motor-cyclist.

"I'd get that headlamp seen to as soon as possible,. Sir!" grunted the policeman, handing him the chrome rim. "Don't want any more accidents, now, do we? And mind how you go. I'll not bother wi' a statement on this one; right?"

I got two thumbsticks from the antlers (my first -.I never could find cast antler in the woods), also a pair of hairy handles from the rear feet as a bonus. The venison wasn't too bad, either, but you have to hang it a bit. Wasn't quite in season, either, of course. The dogs slept happily on the hide for a bit, but I hadn't cured it properly and it soon started shedding hair.

I wouldn't fancy that ride again, mind, on the old ex-G.P.O. Bantam, with the deer draped round my neck. Nearly had me off a few times when it shifted, *and* I got stabbed in my shoulder with one of the antlers.

Better him nor me, anyroad. Would have come a right cropper if *I*'d hit it with the bike!

9
Picking The Winner

In a perfect world the best stick in the Show would always be the winner. But once you outgrow your nappies, you very soon begin to realise that everything out there is anything but perfect. The best stick doesn't win every time and in some cases is not even placed. And it's no good whingeing; once you have entered your Pride and Joy and it's placed in the rack alongside all of the other hopefuls, it's at the mercy of the Judge. And - it has to be said - once competition enters into it, fair-play often goes out of the window, with the Judge being the offender. But before you begin to disagree with these statements, consider the following scenarios (none of which are imagined):

You have shortlisted three sticks for Best. All meet the judging criteria re craftsmanship, accuracy, artistry, imagination or originality, and balance. All in fact are of equal merit. But here lies the problem - one is by someone with whom you share a mutual antipathy; another is by a maker unknown to you; the last is by a friend of yours. Now be honest - who do you think will win?

You have been given a lift to a distant show by a competitor. One of his sticks is in the running. He has a temper on a very short fuse, and likes to win always - you might well be finding your own way home afterwards unless he does well. Again, would you give Best to someone else? If he happens to be a friend it isn't really a problem - you would almost certainly choose his stick anyway.

The possible class winners are all dog-heads, one being a Border Terrier. Bearing in mind that you are the owner of two of this breed it is not difficult to imagine which entry will be the winner.

Finally; one of the possibles is a character who is to judge at a later show where you will be competing yourself. It is inevitable that you will be just a weeny bit naughty and favour him. You will then be a member of the Backscratchers' Brigade. This is quite a fair sized body.

Show committees often exhibit a complete lack of commonsense in selecting Judges. They habitually ask a well-known winning competitor to officiate, quite often for no other reason than to prevent him winning again that year! This is a lamentable state of affairs, but all too common. One stickmaking organisation has a small panel of judges, all committee members, and all competitors themselves (and all founder members of the Backscratchers). For several years I amused myself by accurately predicting the winners of their shows once I knew who was judging that year. The only one I got wrong was when the judge, a farmer, travelled to the show with the eventual winner, a neighbouring farmer, who had only just recently joined their association.

It is just as easy to predict at certain shows who *won't* win, irrespective of how good their sticks are. Certain local shows, commonly in the Borders and the Dales, invariably have local winners. They profess to be "Open" shows, and will happily accept all entries, wherever you live, but "outsiders" can forget about winning - that is for the locals. Nothing intrinsically wrong in that, but the show schedules should stipulate that competitors must reside within x-miles of the showground. That would be more honest - but would reduce entries considerably, of course. One local show-schedule states that all competitors must reside in the county. All very laudable you may feel, except that in this case the showground is three miles from the county boundary. Thus competitors can travel thirty miles or more from the south of the county but not from just over the river, one-tenth of that distance!

You will hear the argument that judges often know competitors' individual style of stick. This is usually correct in the fancy sections, but rather more difficult to differentiate in the plain classes. Many good stickmakers are innovative, regularly coming up with new ideas - and will usually be turning out new, and therefore unseen, sticks each year. Naturally, after a few shows, these sticks *will* become known, but perhaps not for two or three months.

Top-notch stickmakers do not automatically turn out to be good judges; often being rather stereotyped in their ideas and styles, and often looking for sticks rather similar to their own. How often does a wood-stick win Best, for instance? Most judges are "horn happy" and will always go for horn-heids. Nothing wrong in that perhaps, but there are some excellent wood-sticks to be seen. From a show angle, too, I'd much rather see the elite competing than judging. Like other stickmakers, and the Public, I like to see their sticks. It is not essential for the judge to have officiated previously. They have to wet their toes some time! Really a lot of it is quite simply commonsense, assuming that they know something about sticks, and usually carry one, perhaps. After that it's simply down to which stick one likes the most, having regard to the usual criteria. And if favour *is*, or is thought to have been, shown, put yourself in the judge's shoes. Would you have acted any differently? If you can say so truthfully, genuinely, honestly, hand-on-heart virtually nearly positively, all I can say is that you have missed your vocation; you would surely be made welcome in most religious orders.

Don't get the idea from this that all stick-judging is rife with favouritism, nepotism, bias and downright narrow-minded ignorance. It isn't - at least not all of the time.. And never forget that very, very few shows indeed have one absolutely outstanding stick that has *Best* written all over it. There are nearly always at least three or four others that could justifiably claim that accolade, and the great pity is that only one gets the verdict. As they say in certain sports, "Second is nowhere".

Best of luck, then, if you are showing. Mind, strictly-speaking, luck shouldn't enter into it. But it does. When you think about it, only two people usually agree with the decision at a show - the judge and the winner.

10
King Billy

Obviously not all goats live long enough to die of old-age, and this applies even more to wild ones than domesticated. There are an estimated 10,000 of the former in Great Britain, mainly in Wales and Scotland. They are social animals, like sheep, and tend to live in herds. The older billies normally keep together in small groups except for the time of the autumn rut. Occasionally lone billies, usually the deposed 'king' billy, will wander miles away from their home territory at that time. This is the story of one which died from 'lead poisoning', which, as it happened, only anticipated a natural death by a few days...

Gordon was the stalker at Glen Roy, near Spean Bridge, and a very skilled stickmaker, working in the main with Blackface tup-horn and Highland Cow-horn. I usually obtained antler from him, with odd horns thrown in as a bonus, and this year I had asked him if there were any wild goats on the estate.

He said that the nearest herd was some thirty miles away "Ower the hill" on a neighbouring estate, where a friend of his, Sandy, was the stalker. Some four years earlier, an old piebald billy had turned up at Glen Roy in the late autumn, "Looking as if it had been in the wars. "There was a running sore on its neck, its beard was heavily matted with blood and it was limping badly.

Nonetheless, coming lower down the glen with the deer, he survived the winter, feeding quite happily amongst them, on the fodder put out. Gordon had mentioned this billy to Sandy, and he identified it as the former 'king' billy of the herd on his estate. It had enjoyed this status for the past seven or eight years until deposed after several fierce battles with one of his mature sons in the rut. He had obviously chosen not to hang around on the fringe of the herd as most older billies normally do, but wandered off on his own and had apparently made his way to Glen Roy. He was then about sixteen or seventeen years old, and possessed a thirty-inch pair of horns running back over his shoulders in a sweeping curve.

Gordon had harboured designs upon those horns a few times, he admitted. But he reckoned he would get them eventually. "The ould bugger couldn't last that long, in any case." But it was three years after its arrival, when it would then be about twenty years old, that it finally looked to be just about on its last legs. Its head was downcast, it had developed a deep cough, and could hardly walk. Nor was it doing much feeding. All in all it looked as if Gordon was going to get his horns, and he was all set to put it out of its misery when he received a 'phone call from Sandy - "Is th'ould billy still around?"

"Only just," replied Gordon, "but not for verra long, noo."

"Aa hev a German stalker staying," said Sandy. "Got him a 'Royal' (twelve pointer) stag trophy-heid he's having stuffed, and he's getting reet worked up at the chance for a billy goat heid. What ye call 'goat fever', they reckon. An' he's not having the king billy oot o' my herd here. Take that ould bugger up the hill in the morn, and prop him up in some heather where ye canna see what state he's in. We'll be there sharp after breakfast. And we'll mek the bugger work for it!"

Gordon did as requested. Early next morning he trussed up the old billy and took him up the hill in the ATV. Then he manhandled him into a patch of deep heather and left him there. "Looked quite lifelike, aal things considered, even though he had his heid doon." Sandy and the German sportsman, who was resplendent in Tyrolean loden suit and feathered hat, arrived an hour later. The two stalkers immediately set off with him up the steep brae behind Gordon's cottage, taking a route well away from where the goat stood. The German was to get his trophy the hard way.

They gave him, Gordon said, "a reet guid stalk" around the hill at least twice, dropping down 1500 feet, then immediately back up again, two or three times across the burn, and once up the middle of it for 30-40 yards. Then a final, slow, long drawn out crawl across a rough scree slope, with Gordon telling the German to keep his "bluidy big airse" down.

"Sticking up like a hoose-end it was. A stag would hev been in the next coonty afore he got within half a mile. Calls hisself a stalker! Just aboot run his airse off, anyway."

Finally after three hours, he was brought, near exhausted, to within a hundred yards of where the geriatric goat still stood, just where Gordon had left it that morning. His head still drooped but Gordon explained that he was feeding.

Sandy slid the rifle forward to Gordon, who in turn passed it on to the German with the whispered orders: "Wait 'til ye get your wind back, sight on a hundred yards and put it just aback of the shoulder. And keep your bluidy airse doon, man!"

He fired in due course and the billy folded up into the heather at the first shot. As Gordon said, he looked a "richt picture" with his long shaggy beard, fierce amber eyes and magnificent horns, even though "he'd a been deid afore the week was oot, onnyroad."

The German was overjoyed with his trophy, which was to go to the taxidermist at Fort William that same day. ("Better him nor me," said Gordon, "you should ha' smelled it. Fair lifting. Wouldna' like to travel back with it in me luggage either; ye'd get some funny looks aalricht. Not that any daft bugger'd sit next to ye!") The exuberant German had then pulled out his wallet and counted out £300, with Gordon and Sandy trying hard to look nonchalant about the windfall.

"No' bad at all," said Gordon, "for a manky aad billy. Wish we had anither wan or two aboot at that money - mind ye, aa could ha' made a reet fine pair of crooks wi' them horns!"

Spoken like a true stickmaker.

Sandy told Gordon later that the German had asked him "What is this 'airse', he say - is it the head?"

11
So You Fancy Being A Judge

A fairly well-known stickmaking association announce that they are to hold a "Seminar for Novice Judges". This was to be on the lines of master and pupil, with "Experts" and "Novices" on a one to one basis. As one familiar with some of the judging at their shows, where favouritism and backscratching are the norm, the idea suggests certain comic possibilities. I can see the scene now.

"Right, lad, I'm your Expert, and you'll be the Novice, like. You fancy being a Judge like me, then, do you? Seen you round the shows, I reckon, but I don't suppose you've got amongst the rosettes yet. Anyhow it's a great life, I can tell you, this feeling of power you have. There's plenty lads wished they hadn't entered the show, when I start handling their sticks, and that's a fact. You could say you're King for the day. Let me give you a bit of good advice though, mind, - it's not as easy as you think.

First off, soon as you get to the show, make sure you meet the Chairman. If you know him it's "Mr. --". No first names. Otherwise it's "Sir". Take him to the beer-tent soon as you can. If he can't get away, give him a few swigs of your hip-flask. He'll probably talk a load of rubbish, they all do, but try to look like you're paying attention, anyroad; and agree with everything he says. And laugh at his jokes, naturally. Tell him you enter your own sticks in shows, of course, and he'll make sure you'll win regularly from now on.

When you start judging the sticks, listen to the Steward, he'll keep you on the straight and narrow. He knows who all the sticks belong to - if you haven't had time to check up on the entries aforehand yourself, that is. Don't want the prizes going to any bugger in off the street who fancies his chances, now do we? Never mind what their sticks are like. And try to look intelligent, even if you aren't. But not worried, though, and never scratch your head, or you'll look as if you don't know what you're doing. You can scratch your backside, though.

And whatever else, don't drop any of the sticks if you can help it. All them fancy bits are just stuck on usually you know, and are buggers for breaking off.

If you see any sticks from somebody you don't like, pick them up two or three times. Drag it out a bit, he'll think he's in with a shout. Then put them back in the rack... Make sure he's not down to judge any shows you are going to enter, of course. In that case, give him Best.

Now then, we'll have a few questions about these sticks I've got here. How do you rate this one?"

"Well, it's a fish, like. Pike, maybe, with that jaw? Can't say I fancy it - if I pulled that out, I reckon the cat could have it. Bit dead and stiff looking, anyroad."

"Keep your voice down, lad. That was made by him over there, that Expert baffling yon Novice. Pike! Supposed to be a bloody trout, isn't it? Uses it as a model at night-classes for them to copy. Stiff looking! Dead!! Course the bugger is; so would you be if you'd been in the freezer this last twelve-month. Didn't expect him to have a live one on the workbench in a goldfish-bowl, did you? Pay right attention to it anyroad - got a trout-class at our shows now. Mind, they all look like that one; apart from the colours, that is. Steward'll tell you which ones to pick. Now then, what do you make of this?"

"Not much cop. Nose is out of line, and it's got a poor joint. Varnish has run as well. Wouldn't give it house-room myself."

"Dropped yourself right in it, then, haven't you! Made by one of the Committee. Won a few shows that has. You'll have to give it Best-in-Class at least. What about this next one?"

"It's a real cracker, now, this one, isn't it! One of the best I reckon I've ever seen. Best-in-Class and Best-in-Show, no trouble. What a stick!"

"Wrong again, lad. Stick belongs to me. Bought it off one of our members, lives way down in the backwoods, think it's one of them clapped out places in the Midlands, somewhere. He put it in two or three of our shows but never got placed. But it's a cracking stick alright, you're right there; that's why I bought it. But we can't have these buggers coming to the shows from the back of beyond out of the area and winning, can we now, members or not. That's why we always have pre-entry shows, so we know where they are all coming from...

Last stick, now. What do you reckon to this one?"

"Well, let's see, now. Crack or two in the horn; white's showing through; droopy nose and dog-leg in the shank. Should have left the bugger at home!"

"Sorry, lad, forgot to mention; belongs to the Chairman."

"Oh well, now that I've had another look at it; it's a real Bobby Dazzler - I'd give it Best, no hesitation."

"Right, lad; his garage-door's covered with rosettes that this one's won. Bloody awful stick, you're right there - but mind, I didn't say so! Got to get something for being Chairman, I suppose. Anyway, reckon you can go places as a Judge. We'll make a bloody good Backscratcher out of you. Next month you'll be judging that show where I'll be putting some of mine in. I'll tell you which ones they are before the show. Here's your badge. Welcome to the Club."

12
Tup Tales 1 - The Wild Tup

On holiday on the Isle of Arran, Alec the gamekeeper at Brodick Castle (who dabbled a bit in sticks himself) told me of the sixteen-year-old Blackface tup that was living wild in one of the glens in the north of the island. He had seen it himself on several occasions but never, unfortunately when he had the rifle with him! Several attempts had been made to capture it, but it had just dunted out of its path the herd's collies, and the keeper's labrador on one occasion, and headed back up the rocky corries where it was quite at home. Once it had even attacked a hill-walker's terrier and left it bruised and no doubt more than a little frightened. The walker reported that it had just "flattened" his dog when it charged, and he was no doubt glad that it had just continued on and not turned on him! The collies and the labrador were called off when they made to chase it, as it was still very agile for its age and would make a formidable opponent in a face-to-face encounter, especially on its home ground.

Its horns were magnificent, said Alec, and at that age would no doubt be just about near enough solid with next to no gowk or core. A stickmaker's dream, although possibly the restrictions on its diet might affect the strength of the horn, unless it had access to any mineral licks on its forays down the glen. It had escaped to the hills eight years previously and been seen frequently in the company of a small herd of red deer stags. Alec said that there was talk of trying to persuade one of the German or Belgian stalkers who visited the island annually, that this was in fact undoubtedly a wild animal and would present the unique opportunity for a fine trophy head. They were "trophy mad" he said, and this tup would make a fine specimen, with its long unkempt hair, fierce amber eyes and, of course, those horns. And it would cost the sportsman £250, no less, which was an astronomical figure compared with its value at the mart! If we can't get a stalker to take him, said Alec, he'd be just as happy letting him live out his life. He was confident that the eagles, buzzards and ravens would soon let him know the where and when after it died, and he'd have the horns.

"Mind ye," he added, "he wouldna' be onny guid on 'One Man And His Dog'. The dog hasna' been born that'd get thon bugger in a pen!"

Actually, a tup living wild is not such a rare occurrence in hill country. I found a skeleton of one once, horns and all, in a gully in the Lake District, and heard of another in upper Teesdale found in similar circumstances. A friend who has farming relatives in Wales once sent me a photograph of a hefty pair of horns removed from a dead tup which had been living wild for several years on a steeply-wooded hillside in the upper Wye Valley. Hardy hill breeds of sheep can survive where few other animals can, in harsh weather conditions and on a poor diet, and no doubt the lure of the wild can be quite strong, as they have retained enough of their wild instincts to exist without any help from man.

Tup Tales 2 - The Dead Tup

In my pocket I have a rough sketch-map of my destination, given me last night by a hiking friend. I find myself chuffing up a steep hillside in the Lake District. Thankfully there's a well used sheep trod going my way but it's still a hell of a pull. I go on and up through the heather, wondering why sheep's feet, like those of deer, are so close together, the trod being hardly more than six inches wide. I'm puffing and wheezing, with me gob so dry that I don't have enough spit left to lick a second-class postage-stamp. Anyway this must be that big round boulder he's marked on the map. Nearly there. Another steep pull and it levels off slightly and I stop thankfully to take my bearings.

A pair of ravens and a buzzard get up from a tumble of rocks across the hillside and I can see the scatter of grey wool. This must be it; so I scramble over the dry-stone dyke snaking away up the hill, and hurry across. And so it proves; the Herdwick tup is virtually down to skin and bone - but what a pair of horns! The teeth are worn to stumps and he was obviously an old one; probably did a runner a few years back and had since been living rough. Somebody has been trying to cut through one horn with a knife, there's a shallow notch nibbled into the base. The blade will need sharpening now, that's for sure. You can cut with the grain on horn with a knife after a fashion but you're an optimist trying to cut across it. I soon have the whole skull away and tie it to the outside of my old army-haversack and head back down. It's not only the descent which is making me step-out lively!

Later on in the summer I'm at one of the local shows and there are a few of the lads listening to Big Charlie rabbiting on. Bony red fizzog; horse-blanket-check tweed suit; lanky (could hide behind a lamp post); loud voice and always whingeing. Good stickmaker but a real pain in the fundament. I hear the word "Pike" and draw a little closer (the tup had been on the Pike). "Got reet up t'fellside, must ha' bin three or fower mile (nearer two), then fund I'd left me saw ahint. Tried wi' me knife but buggered it up (I knew it). Went back agin next day but they'd gone. Some bugger'd had them away. Thievin' sods!"

Fair made my day!

Tup Tales 3 - One Off

It was a favourite walk of mine when I lived in the Lake District; nice scenery, and away from all the hordes of tourists. The old packhorse-track up the valley had been worn down by constant use over the years, to a level well below the surrounding land. In its lower reaches it was a sunken lonnen, hemmed in for a few hundred yards by the hanging roots of hawthorn, hazel, ash and rowan, whilst higher up the fellside it became more rocky and not so well-defined, but still easy enough to follow.

I had usually managed one or two sticks from those bushes and this late Autumn day had been no exception. A good right-angle handle root-ash with an interesting kink where the root had grown around a stone. Possibilities there, I was sure. Better still, a nice hefty hazel-block which would make a grand crook. I tucked both away vertically, out of sight I hoped, in the middle of a bush, put a large pebble on a flat rock as a marker, and pushed on towards the open fell.

Just as the last bush was left behind I stopped to admire a bunch of tups in the field below. Swaledales all, and a fine show of horn, more than you could shake a stick at. A mouth-watering sight for any stickmaker. The majority were bunched together over the far side, odd pairs squaring off and dunting each other, the rest milling about restlessly, frustrated no doubt, waiting for the coming nuptials. Two were away from the others, just below me, and one seemed to be feeding, its muzzle pushed through wire-mesh stretched between two stakes across a short gap in the dry-stone dyke. It kept trying to shake its head yet seemed to be in difficulties. I had a brief look through my pocket binoculars and fancied that one horn had hooked in the mesh. So I went down to lend a hand.

It had somehow managed to get *both* horns through the six-inch mesh, either by head-rubbing or trying to reach some succulent bite on the far side and naturally when its horns had both curled back around the mesh it hadn't a hope. I tried pushing its head a little forward to ease the strain but the awkward bugger resisted strongly, pulling back with all its might. Next I tried pulling to one side only, thinking that I might work a single horn free. No joy. Then I had my brainwave; if I cut off a horn with my pruning-saw I should manage - hopefully - to release the other one. There was a sudden thumping noise behind me and next thing I know I received a terrific dunt in the backside that flung me arse over tip (or arse over *tup*, in this case!) across the animal with my head wedged up against the mesh. If I hadn't been wearing my heavy tweed cap my head would probably have been wedged through the far side also. Bugger; what had hit me?

I scrambled around and there was the other tup I'd forgotten about, standing three or four yards away with lowered head and stamping forefoot. The sod was ready to have another go! I sat on the haunch of the tup I was entangled with - he was in no position to object - drew back my legs and when he charged this time he got a pair of size-seven Commando-soles right on the nose. Fat lot of good that did me, wedged up back against the mesh. And the sod was all lined up again ready for yet another try. You could see how the word rambunctious got into the language.

Then I had my second inspiration. What was I doing mucking around on *this* side of the mesh anyway when I could do the necessary from the far side where the horns were? So I got over double-quick. Of course this time when I tried to pull the tup's head a mite further through the mesh he resisted strongly, bracing himself and heaving backwards. So I would have to saw as best I could, just as it was. I locked the saw blade and put both hands through the mesh, holding one horn-tip firmly in my left and trying to get a good angle for sawing with the other. Buggerit, his ear was in the way! Then, after a little think about it, another good idea. I pulled off my neckerchief and with a bit of wangling managed to work it around his head and over his ear and tied it down firmly. Looked like an illustration from a Beatrix Potter book.

Halfway through sawing I sensed some movement out of the corner of my eye and just managed to pull my arms back to my side of the mesh before Buggerlugs charged again. This time he hit the mesh only. One or two more efforts like that and I fancied that another tup would be hung up on the wire. I set to again with the saw and managed to zip off the horn without any further trouble. Then it was only the work of a minute or two to untangle the other horn and push the head free. The tup got up from his knees and walked away a bit unsteadily, shaking his head. No doubt his balance would be a bit shaky for a day or two. He looked bloody ridiculous in that neckerchief. Oh Hell! I'd forgotten entirely about that. Not a hope of getting it back now. Still, being philosophical, not a bad swap, I suppose. As I walked back down the track a few minutes later I looked over the bankside into the field. All the remaining tups were gathered about the freed one now - perhaps admiring his kerchief. The consolation of course was that, having helped an animal in trouble, I'd been well rewarded for my efforts.

I'd love to know what the shepherd made of it when he saw it - one horn missing and a kerchief around its head. Hope he got to remove it before any neighbours saw it. Can just imagine the chuff he'd have to put up with otherwise:

"Reckon it'll fetch more at t'Mart, then, tarted up like that!?"

"Is yon tup o' yours ailing, then? Thon wi' the red spotty hanky roond its heid. Got toothache, then, has it!?"

A thought did cross my mind on the way home - if I'd kept my wits about me (a mite difficult admittedly, what with wrestling with one tup *and* trying to avoid the charges of the other demented bugger) then I could have had the *other* horn, too!

Sheep when frightened lose control of both bowel and bladder (They aren't alone in this!). I had been scrambling around for some time in a glutinous mess of sheep-shit. The strides I had on that day were best Army Surplus Stores "Barrack Dress Trousers". These can be recommended for fairly smart and certainly presentable country/casual wear, being Perma-Press and in fine worsted. The colour is a rather nice olive shade. Fortunately this is not too dissimilar to what I had been rolling in. The smell was something else. The Gaffer flatly refused to put them in the washer, so I soaked them in the greenhouse water-tank for a week. The indoor chrysanthemums were particularly good that year!

13
Show Time

Once the swifts and the swallows head South the keen competitor will start to spend long hours in his workshop. Whether it be barn, shed, cellar, back-bedroom, kitchen-table or under-stairs-cupboard, he will be slaving away on his entries for the next season's shows. Country shows are proliferating nowadays, to such an extent that there is slight chance of any new show succeeding if its date clashes with another, already-established one in the area. This recently happened at Castle Howard in Yorkshire where a new Country Fair ran for two years before giving up. The venue was first-class, reasonably central in an area of high population and had every indication that it would develop into a popular show. Unfortunately the organisers had not reckoned on the counter-attraction on the same weekend of the traditional and loyally-supported nearby Northallerton Show. Stick-competitions are held at the majority of these shows and any keen stickmaker, whether competing or simply admiring - or picking up new ideas - could probably attend a show virtually every week from May through to October.

The ardent competitor will have put in innumerable hours in his workshop before the surrendering of his treasures to the merciless scrutiny of the show-judge (not to mention the spectators). Whether in a muddy cowpat-splattered field, back-room of a pub or village-hall, or in the grounds of some stately-home with show-ring events, a vast array of trade-stands and an attendance of thousands, the entries will provoke passions and pleasure that will range from friendly rivalry to downright rage, envy, and bitter jealousy. They will meet, greet, eat and compete - some will even cheat. Many will feel compelled afterwards (some with justification) to bleat. Quite a few will reckon that they stand towards the judge as a lamp post does towards a dog.

What makes a competitor do it? Everyone has, to some degree, an inbuilt urge to compete, and no doubt this is usually triggered off by seeing prize-winning entries at some show and thinking, "I can do better than that." Generally they will graduate through the smaller local shows to the big hotly contested ones, where competitors may travel considerable distances, and often also require overnight-accommodation to attend. Entries can range from a few dozen to several hundred.

Contestants come in two distinct categories. The dedicated usually follow the show-circuit and travel with no less than ten, and sometimes up to thirty, of their best creations and enter as many as the regulations allow, or common sense - and rival entries - dictate, allowing for the known whims or fancies of the judge, and the strength of the opposition on the day. Many however have just a few sticks from which to make a choice; they may not often win, but admirably, they are willing to have a go. In one sense, having the two levels of contestant in the same show can be considered unfair competition, but I can think of several instances of an unknown entering his first show with only two or three sticks, and being awarded Best-In-Show. The regular winners have to accept that when they compete in smaller local shows, there is occasional resentment from the more modest competitor at being up against the experts. The latter are in fact helping to raise the standards, and as stated earlier, there is always the chance of an occasional upset. Entrants also feel, of course, that they should support the activities of their own association, and they like to compete against members on a friendly(!) basis. Not that it always turns out that way.

I wouldn't pretend to know what drives the regular competitor to do it, but he must have a well developed competitive instinct, combined with an understandable desire to exhibit good craftsmanship. Certainly it is not for the prizes; the rosette pinned so proudly on the wall or workshop door will only have cost the show organisers a few pence. Naturally if you are selling sticks, however, the addition of a show rosette can put up the asking price considerably. I have even heard of cases where they have been bought in especially for the occasion.

14
How Long Is A Stick?

Experts are often self-appointed, and feel compelled to make their views known. Their speculative and exaggerated opinions coupled with sweeping statements, brooking no argument, tend to dupe rather than educate. Their advice, given with such pontifical certitude is best treated with a healthy degree of scepticism. Expect a diarrhoea of words but a constipation of practical ideas.

The stickmaker had been in conversation with an "Occupational Therapist". (Now there's a title for you; about on a par with others such as "Rural Environment Services Officer" or "Post Traumatic Stress Syndrome Counsellor". All grandiose job titles and dubious qualifications). He had been informed by this pundit that "so many people have their sticks the wrong size", and then received instructions regarding the "accepted" method to ensure the "correct" size. Apparently one had to "stand straight with relaxed shoulders and arms held loosely by the sides". The stick is to be held upside down with the handle on the ground and the shank is marked at the point level with the *ulna* or *radius styloid.* (This is meaningless waffle or "blinding you with science" - the ulna and radius are the two bones of the forearm, and the styloid is the protruding end of the bone at either side of the wrist in this instance. Now why could that not have been explained in simple English?) The shank is then sawn off at the marked point.

It is obvious that all that this lay-down-the-law type knows about stickmaking could be written down on the back of a postage-stamp with a Magic-Marker. I'll give you some very sound advice of my own (and I've been carrying a stick since about the time I started to learn joined-up writing). If you follow all this rigmarole you will find that you have buggered up what was no doubt a perfectly good length stick. I tried myself out for size as detailed and found that, following the fatuous advice given, I would be left with a stick all of 32 inches in length! It's just a pity that such silly sods don't try out these daft ideas before recommending them.

I regularly meet two old gaffers walking down the road. Both carry sticks. The taller of the two has a shortish blackthorn thumbstick, at most three-and-a-half-foot long perhaps, whilst his "marrer" carries a four-foot-six-inch long shoulder-height horn-crook. I stopped for a crack one day and we got on about sticks, naturally. "Look at yon," said Thumbstick, "thinks he's still up on t'farm with that bloody big sheep-stick, and him retired ten years sin'!" "Hark at him," said the vertically-challenged one (sorry, the jargon must be catching - the shorter one, I meant) "wi' thon twig of his. Seen fairies in t'pantomime wi' bigger wands than yon. An' them just bairns, an' all!"

This puts the whole length position into perspective. At least a foot difference between the two sticks and both owners quite happy in their choice. Neither did they require the services of any "expert" to tell them what length stick they should have had. The best stick-length for anyone is simply the length that one feels happy with. [No words of more than two syllables there - nor do you need a dictionary.]

15
Booty From The Car Boot

"How much?" says I, holding it up.

"A pound, I reckon," she says; perhaps a shade hesitantly.

"Give you fifty-pence."

"Seventy-five."

"Right!" says I, delighted.

What I had just acquired was a brass-backed "Superior Grade" Marples ten-inch tenon-saw. It had a light coating of rust but the blade was not pitted and none of the points were broken Indeed, it scarcely needed sharpening by the look of it, having obviously seen little use. The current tool-catalogue price is between £40-£50 depending where you are buying. This one was with a bundle of rusted hardware items in a cardboard-box under the trestle-table. I ended up with half-a-dozen assorted jubilee-clips (useful for horn-work) and handed over £1. The vendor appeared quite satisfied with the sale!

It was just one of quite a few bargains that I've had over the past year at a local car-boot-sale. This one started perhaps two years ago and is now the largest in the area with between 200-300 vendors each week between Easter and early-November. The venue is the local rugby-ground, and is becoming more and more popular. There is another even larger one held on a racecourse twentyfive miles away. Here, and at the local traditional street-markets, you can find for sale at one time or another, a vast variety of items from toys to tools. Certainly if I were setting up a kit of tools for a workshop nowadays, I doubt if I could get the basic essentials for less than £500. This might seem a bit over the odds, but not if you reckon that a decent handsaw and tenon-saw would set you back at least £100 for the pair nowadays. A decent-quality chisel or gouge would be around £10, with rasps twice as much. For the same items at a car-boot-sale, if you know what you are after, and can recognise good quality when you see it, despite rust and grime, you can pick up many of these items for around £1 each. They will probably require a bit of work on them, often rust-removal and perhaps sharpening, but older tools are invariably made from superior materials to modern ones and are well worth the effort in finding and renovating them.

Naturally everyone likes a bargain and these can certainly be had at the car-boot sale or the market. You can sometimes even get decent horn of various sorts - mainly cow-horn but occasionally big-game trophies or deer-antlers You may find other items of interest such as narwhal or walrus tusks which are actually ivory. So too for that matter were old billiard and snooker balls, but you must be able to distinguish those from later resin ones. Obviously these are not often seen about, although the balls aren't too uncommon. One lives in hope! I don't think that I have ever come away from a sale without having bought something of interest, and with an entry fee of 30p you are hardly out of pocket in any case.

You must be prepared to plough through a load of clothing, toys, footwear and junk of all descriptions; but you may just find that nugget amidst all the dross. I know that I was chuffed recently when rooting through an old tin of coins on a stall for wren-farthings, which I'm rather partial to, mainly for capping out cut-edges on antler. I found a silver Eire threepenny-piece, 1960-ish, with a lovely relief of a sitting hare on one face. Price? - One penny! As it happens, I bought other things that morning but I would have been quite happy with just that coin. As a matter of interest I've since acquired other Irish coins; there's a nice red-deer stag, and a leaping salmon, also a pig, and a hen and chickens. So if you were making a stick for a stalker, fisherman or farmer, they are all ideal to personalise it.

The best areas for all tools are those with an industrial conurbation. The recession has meant that thousands of items from factories and works have been rendered obsolete, and many, as a matter of course, find their way down into the markets. Industrial or professional-grade of tools of any description are naturally superior to the D.I.Y. type normally available.

The old saying, "One man's junk is another man's treasure" certainly refers. But keep away from "my" local car boot sale!

16
Sensayuma

I was at this country-show and bumped into an old friend, Shuggy. He's a stickmaker, too, and a good one, so naturally we ended up at the Stick Tent. Neither of us had entered any sticks that day, so we felt free to indulge in that favourite stickmaker's pastime, criticising the O.B.E. (Other Buggers' Efforts). The judging had just finished and the winning sticks, all sporting their rosettes, made a colourful display on the winner's stand.

"What d'you reckon to Best-in-Show, Shug?" says I. "Think it's meant to be a trout? Look at the jaw on it. Seen better looking pike. Bloody awful."

"Dunno," says Shuggy, "could even be a salmon. Not much cop, that's for sure. The colour of it! If I caught one like that I'd put the bugger back, wouldn't fancy eating it, like."

The spectator to the right of me, the one with the flat-cap, fat red face and matching neck, snorted at this but didn't say anything.

"Look at thon shank there," says Shuggy, "the bugger's like a dog's hind-leg."

I agree, "Nice handle; lovely bit of horn, pity about the shank. Bet it was never taken out of the rack, or if it was, he only looked at the handle. It's not just bent, that shank, bugger's got a kink in it. Right up next the handle. Spoils the look of it."

Cloth-Cap looks a bit redder in the face, but still never says anything, although he looks on the verge.

"What about this 'un then? Bit long in the nose, and it's rat-tailed."

"Never liked that style, meself. Should be a bit of a curve to the neb. Must be three inches of straight there, *and* it drops below the joint."

"Get a look at those sloping joints as well. What's the point, do you reckon?"

"Dunno, just trying to show how clever they are, probly. Spoils the look of them. Not as good as level ones, anyroad."

Cloth-Cap seems to mutter something, but I can't hear what he says. He might be talking to his neighbour.

"Norra bad badger, like, but should have more grey in it," says Shuggy, "he's striped it like a zebra."

"Eyes too far back," I fancy, "and jaws too narrow. Chin isn't white either; more like grey as you say. Thon's a good fox though. Pity he's got the colour wrong."

After a second scrutiny we both agree that the ears too are a bit on the small side and shouldn't be facing forward, either.

"Reckon they've been stuck on, anyway," I say.

"Must ha' been," says Shuggy, "couldn't see horn that thick."

"Wouldn't be surprised if this winner is a relative of the Judge."

"Or mebbe travelled to t'Show with him. More than likely offered to *take* him!"

Cloth-Cap turns to both of us now, his face nearly purple. "Two clever-buggers, aren't you?" He was fair spluttering with rage.

"Tell you this; yon fish-stick of mine has won a few shows, so there's nowt wrong with it; and that shank's meant to have a kink in it, it's a Patterdale crook. And I *like* a long straight nose, *and* a sloping joint, and thon badger and fox were copied off stuffed ones! And nowt's stuck on, either! Put yer own sticks up and see if you do any better."

Shuggy and I both agree that if that fish has won before then he's either a relative of the Judge, or he follows him around the shows where he's judging. Both probably Backscratchers, more than like.

A few weeks later both of us are at another show, and are just entering our sticks when Cloth-Cap comes into the marquee.

"Yon's the Judge the day," says the Steward, and we both keep our backs turned so he doesn't recognise us.

"Doubt if he's got a Sensayuma," says Shuggy, "so best if he doesn't see us."

I get an odd rosette or two, but Shuggy has a field-day with three Firsts and Best-in-Show. Cloth Cap doesn't seem to remember me when he presents the prizes but I see that quite a few words pass between him and Shuggy, who comes over afterwards with his trophy.

"Wouldn't shake me hand, when he saw who it was. Said I wouldn't have won if he'd known it was me. Cheeky bugger! So I telled him 'All mine have straight joints. No kinks in the shank, either, and the noses are shorter and curved. *And* a good few bits and pieces have been stuck on here and there including the one that got Best!' Then I said he was nowt but an apology for a Judge. Should ha' seen his fizzog. Neck swelled up like a turkey-cock! Thowt he was going to blow a gasket! We'd best steer clear of him after this. No Sensayuma at all!"

17
An A-Z of Stickmaking

A = Apple. This is classified in the trade as fruitwood, along with cherry, crab, damson, pear and plum. All are good for carving, with a fine even grain. Occasionally decent shanks can be had, although the taper is usually a mite drastic, but there is nothing special about them. Plum will often resemble blackthorn in bark-colouration but the others are fairly nondescript.

B = Bodge. The art of mixing horn-, antler- or wood-dust with glue to effect (hopefully) an invisible repair to some defect, whether hole, crack, or other cavity, usually in a handle. When done by an expert this can be reasonably satisfactory. Likewise when painted over, of course. When done by an amateur can be bloody awful.

C = Collar. This is the essential joint-strengthening between handle and shank. It can be of horn, antler, wood, or metal (ugh!). Without it there is a potential weakness in the joint. Not to be confused with the more common - and purely cosmetic - spacer or washer.

D = Deer-Foot Handles. A hairy handle I find unpleasant to the touch when dry. When wet, it doesn't bear thinking about. Yet, for some reason I can't fathom, they are always popular.

E = Elastoplast. Much in demand amongst stickmakers who use that ridiculous carving tool, the Stanley knife.

F = Ferrule. If you want a ferrule on your stick for serious walking, fit a length of copper or brass piping to the tip. If it's just for twirling around when you go to town, or walk the dog in the park, then by all means fit a fancy one of horn or antler.

G = Grain. A while back I made two rather nice wood-crooks. One was ash with a nice grain in the honey-coloured wood, but enhanced by a lovely watermark stain in a dark walnut shade. The other, a blackthorn (and as a matter of fact the only blackthorn crook that I've seen), had the purplish-red stain in the handle that you normally get just underneath the bark on the wood surface.

Would that I still had both, but alas, in each case I succumbed to an offer that I couldn't refuse.

H = Hole-in-the-horn. You will often encounter tup-horn with a hole bored through, usually near the nose. If small, the hole will often disappear when working the horn. An ingenious solution is to *elongate* the hole lengthways along the horn and to insert a miniature fox, badger, stoat, otter, or trout in horn in the "window". A clever improvisation.

I = Inside Line. Like a lot of other nonsense in stickmaking literature, great faith is placed in fixing the "inside-line" first when shaping a wood- or horn-handle. The truth of the matter is that, if you have any sort of eye at all, it is just as easy to draw the *outside*-line first. An advantage is that you can more readily confine the shape within the limits of the material available .

J = Joint. The joint between handle and shank was originally horizontal. Then some bright bugger, intent no doubt on impressing stick-show judges, started making sloping joints. Now lots of others follow suit. If you are really feeling clever why not try two other types, the zig-zag and the dovetail. The latter is only possible on a horn-handle stick. Succeed with these and you can really feel pleased with yourself. [But don't expect to *improve* the stick by doing so.]

K = Kinks. You have a shank with a kink. The books offer a plethora of advice: Straighten over your knee (try that with holly or blackthorn!); in a vice; in a notched wood "horse"; with a jack. Heat it with a fan-heater; a hot-air gun; a naked flame; a steaming kettle. Cover with foil; sacking; a damp cloth. Your mind reels with the possibilities. I subscribe to none of these methods, but simply chop the stick up and put it on the fire. There are plenty more straight ones where that one came from.

L = Length. Disregard any arbitrary pronouncements in books or articles about "correct" stick length. The proper length for *anyone* is the length that they are most happy with.

M = Mini-Burrs or Galls. These are small blister-like growths on certain trees, varying in size from golf-ball to tennis-ball or larger; and usually encrusted in flaking or cracked bark. After seasoning for a month or two, debark, and you will usually find the most intriguing grain-formation. Quite often the timber has a greenish tinge. Ideal for a carved head for a stick. Most commonly found (up North at least) on oak, cherry, birch and hawthorn. Can be removed easily from the tree by a hammer-blow as a rule but a broad-blade chisel will make a neater job.

N = Nose. The nose on the handle can turn in or out. It can droop (even at Shows!). It can be substantial with a majestic curve - a true Roman nose; or it can be thin and inelegant (again, seen at Shows) - a rat tail of a nose. But unlike the nose on your face, with patience and experience you can learn how to shape it to your heart's desire.

O = Oval. Many older judges disregard sticks with an oval-cross-section shank. This is nonsense. A good proportion of holly, blackthorn and hawthorn have oval shanks, and are none the worse for it. An oval-shaped handle to fit such a shank comes to hand just as easily as a round one and looks equally as good.

P = Pot-Hunters. You have entered your pride and joy in one of the classes at the Show. There are five others in the class so the odds on a place aren't too bad. Then, at the last minute, having weighed up the opposition the Pot-hunter arrives and puts six of his sticks in the class. At a stroke the odds against you have doubled and the P.-H. has derisory odds of perhaps 2 - 1 only against him winning. And all for a rosette. It is not unknown even for these "enthusiasts" to enter two different shows on the same day, sending perhaps half of their sticks on with a friend to enter them on his behalf.

The Welsh have the best solution to the problem. At their shows, entries are limited to one per head per class. The only drawback to this system is that overall entries would drop if it was applied universally. But it would signal the end for the Pot-hunter.

Q = Quaint. A word which describes some of the more outlandish - and quite useless - ornately carved sticks entered in shows. They are but carved ornaments jointed to a shank and masquerading as sticks. They can't be *handled* and let's face it, that's what a handle is for, after all. They are aptly known up North as "wall" or "indoor" sticks. These treasures are transported reverently around the show-circuit, cocooned from harm in bubble-wrap or individual padded covers. I have even seen them for sale on occasion with the notice "Please Do Not Handle" prominent!

R = Repeats. Unless a stick is a "once-off" - and that is a rare bird indeed - I would have no qualms about selling if the offer was good enough. If you can do it once, you can do it again, and often better in the light of experience. I had to smile recently at a magazine-article about a stickmaker disposing of one of his fancy sticks - "As any great artist, he viewed its departure with mixed feelings, glad in a way to see it in good hands, but feeling its loss as keenly as might a mother her child." - No mention at all of the wad of folding nestling in his pocket. Doubtless that should go some way to cushion the shock ... But "mother and child"! Hyperbole at its most nauseating.

S = Sloe Gin. Nothing to do with stickmaking, you may say. But I always get my sloes in November and December when looking for blackthorn-shanks. If you can't find one you can usually manage the other.

T = "Twisty" Sticks. Found where the stick has played host to the honeysuckle which has twined lovingly around the shank and caused the spiral distortion. This is always clockwise and one that isn't has been induced artificially by wrapping twine around a growing young stick (cunning-buggers, stickmakers). There is often a weak-spot somewhere along the length of a "twisty", usually disguised by bark, where the bine has bitten in deeply.

U = Underground. In your haste to cut a good shank don't forget the part that may be underground. A nice root-formation has made many a good handle but naturally you don't know it's there until you look.

V = Varnish. If you intend to sell a stick, varnish the shank by all means. Otherwise use linseed-oil; a well-oiled stick improves with age. A varnished one doesn't.

W = Whoops-Factor. We have all experienced it. The knife, or chisel, drill or other tool suddenly takes on a life of its own and whoops!, you have a cut or gouge-mark where you didn't bargain for. All tools have an inbuilt whoops-factor in greater or lesser degree with the "blue riband" going to that D.I.Y. stalwart, the Stanley knife.

X marks the spot where back in July you saw that lovely straight "silver" hazel, which you left until winter. When you returned in December you found (of course) that some other bugger had beaten you to it.

Y = Yell. This is the sound you utter when you are a dozen feet up a holly tree, and you have just sawn off a nice block stick; only to find that the sawed branch is actually the one you were standing on.

Z = Zenith. The highest peak of happiness. Achieved by the stickmaker when you complete your first horn-head; when you find that blackthorn-thicket bristling with beautiful straight shanks; when the old gaffer presents you with a pair of tup-horns, thick and solid, after you make him a wood-crook; when you find that gully over Rannoch Moor strewn with stag-antler;

when you enter your first stick-show with one stick only and are placed in your class.

Enjoy yourselves!

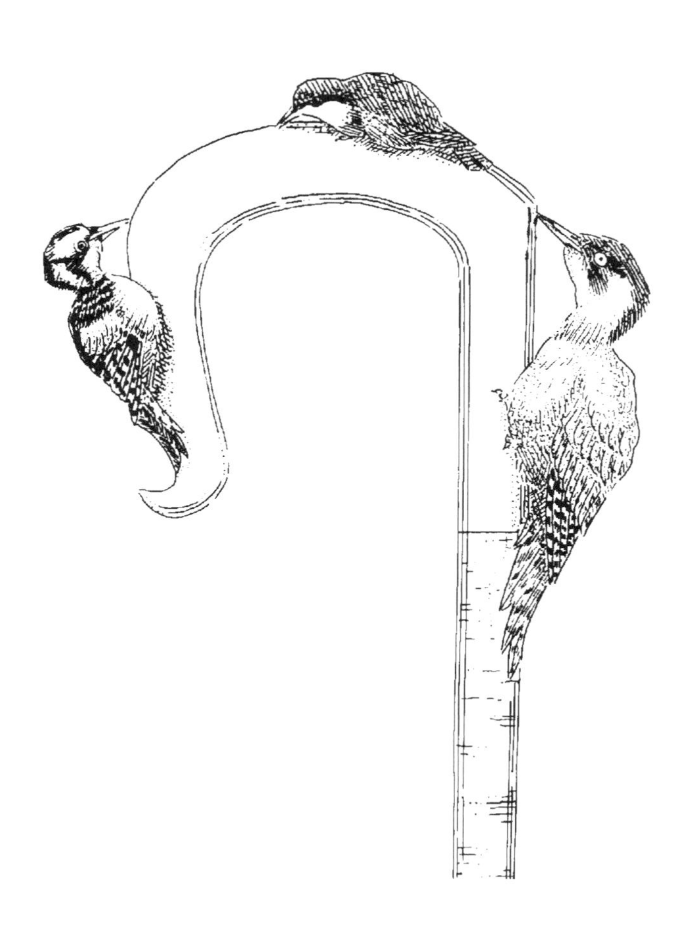

18
That Bloody Judge!

Brogues burnished like conkers today; best cavalry-twills; tweed bum-flapper jacket with horn-buttons; and of course, a tie. "Can't have the judge looking like a badly-lagged water-tank," says the Gaffer. Bait? Flask? Ticket? Car-park pass? Handkerchief? - What it's like to be organised. But I'm off to t'Show eventually.

I'm waved to the front of the queue of vehicles at the entrance and end up right next to the showground. There's an exit nearby; handy if I need to make a quick getaway afterwards!

The Chairman welcomes me - "Keep you busy today, lad - over a hundred racked already." Tell him I'm going for a leg-stretch and promise to be back in good time. Just outside the marquee I bump into a bunch of lads I know and we stop for a jawbone. One starts to unwrap his sticks from a bubblepack-bag saying, "Been busy this winter. Just get a look at these." I grab his arm - "Leave the buggers be. I don't want to see them - yet! They'll all think this is a Backscratchers bloody convention!" He apologises - "Never thought of that! - Reckon they're good'uns, mind." Can't help smiling ... I know what they'll be, alright, sight unseen. He specialises in half-head wildfowl; ducks and geese, with an odd swan-crook occasionally, and they are always "good'uns".

Then I potter around the trade stands, meet a few more of the lads, enjoy the bustle and the crack for a couple of hours, and wander across to the car for a snack. Back at the tent I meet the Steward, an old acquaintance, and just after one-o-clock, away we go.

They say that a keen gardener should have a cast-iron back - with a hinge in the middle. On the other hand, a stick-judge needs only an ability to appreciate a good, or very good, stick. Ideally this should be linked with a sharp eye and selective hearing. The first will let him spot, even in the murk of the marquee, faulty-joints, fallen-arches, twisted-noses and untreated scratches, any of which could have been cured had the owner recognised the ills. The second will enable him to disregard the inevitable comments from spectators, hung over the ropes during judging; ("Having a right good look at that one of mine." or "Whymanyebugger! He's put it back!"). Lurking within tent is a popular pastime at stick-shows, and you can expect a fair bit of this in the course of the afternoon.

We handle every stick as a matter of course. Someone has lavished time and care upon each, and it is simple courtesy to do so. Also, a stick is not just a pretty face. It must be appreciated in its entirety from the neck down. Not all are up to a good standard - if asked to rate some on a scale of one to ten the fairest reply would be - "No comment!" These usually look out of place in a show, standing out like clumps of dandelions in a Best Kept Village. You half expect to see a 'Made in Taiwan' label. Others look like possibilities initially, but are let down by their finish. One is so rough that you could see more bumps than on a Camel Corps patrol. Some of the classes are easy to judge; wood-thumbsticks for instance, particularly if one-piece. The antler-classes too, provide few problems normally, there being a limit to the variations possible. Whilst loth to admit bias, albeit tempered with fairness, there are some pet dislikes. The leaping trout with "tail in line", a rigid straight-from-the-freezer travesty of the real thing; crooks with thistles that lean in or out; and those ever present crooks in the fancy section where life-size birds - blue-tit, wren, nuthatch, woodpecker or kingfisher perch, as big as Sunday-roasts in proportion to the handles, none of which will exceed one-inch in diameter along the shaped length. All will be resident too on that part of the handle where you would naturally grip, and unbalance the overall symmetry.

Black buffalo-horn handles come in mirror-finishes, often looking like plastic, with none of the subtle graduation of shade and colour and texture of other horn, so they end up back in the rack usually. A mallard-head takes the eye ("Bubblepack?") but I don't know why he tiddles around with crescent-shape feathering. In life the drake's head-feathers look so fine that they resemble hair - much easier to do also. But he's set in his ways and won't change - it's like expecting a hedgehog to lay-off traffic.

Final choice is between three similar plain crooks but in different horn. There's nothing between them as far as shape and finish goes, but the reddish cowhorn is given Best, a Jacobs second (the variegated markings a little lopsided; otherwise?) and a slightly bloodshot tup-horn third. They all come to hand easily and would be a pleasure to use. I would love to have made any one of them myself and would most certainly like to be able to take any one home with me. And that is as good a judging criteria as you need after the usual ones have been considered. Is it then as simple as that, a matter of opinion? As a matter of fact, although you might expect more, that *is* it.
The old saying has it. *"He who works with his hands is a labourer; he who works with his hands and his head is a craftsman; but he who works with his hands, his head and his heart is an artist."*
And the stick made by such should win every time.

Most of the lads seem happy enough afterwards. At least one should be very chuffed. The runner-up not quite so much perhaps. The class winners and other rosette-holders will be thinking of what might have been. Whilst for the empty-handed majority, the unsung, uncomplaining foot-soldiers or camp-followers at every show, well, they too can dream - next time... Thankfully, to date, post-traumatic-stress-syndrome has yet to be discovered following stick-shows.

I have a cup of tea and a sandwich back at the car after saying my farewells. I rip car-park and show-stickers off the windscreen, give my Judge's rosette to a youngster standing with his mother by the next car, then take my tie off. Another show over. I wish I could make one like that cowhorn. The bugger *would* shake my hand afterwards, too. Got a nasty look or two there at that, both of us, from some of the other lads.

Two of them pass the car, not seeing me. I hear a snatch of conversation, as they walk by, chewing the fat, "That bloody Judge!" Then I'm off home.

19
Offcuts 1 - The Hazel Corpse

I met one of the local lads in a wood when out with the terriers. The wood had been acquired by the Local Authority as part of its "Countryside Park" complex of woodlands, fields, ponds and streams, and a stretch of river. They boast a team of "Countryside Wardens" - sorry, "Rangers" (they don't care for that word "Warden"), who flit around this "park" in their four-wheel-drive-vehicles, all bearing the 'country park' logo, with few duties that I can see apart from putting up notices with "Footpath" on. Just in case you hadn't noticed where thousands had already trod.

The area where we met up was in a clearing where some Scots pines had recently been felled and cleared. I asked the lad why this had been done, as I understood that the trees were to be left to grow naturally. He said that he had been talking to the local Ranger. (You'll no doubt have met his sort; all NHS type spectacles; beard; green wellies and waxed-cotton jacket - the last two items *de rigueur* whatever the weather or the season. The key words in any conversation with them are invariably "heritage", "ecology", and, inevitably, "environment". They are normally graduates with degrees in Sociology or similar useless subjects, and their binoculars are always at the ready, never cased). The expert informed the lad that his intention was to create a hazel "corpse" (blame the non-local accent!) in the cleared patch of woodland. I was shown a few dozen hazel-twigs planted here and there, all mulched with pine-sawdust. Well, he had his hazel "corpse" alright as the ground thereabouts was stony and sandy, eminently suitable for growing pines, but no good whatsoever for hazel, which prefers a good loam, plenty of leaf-litter, and damp. I noticed, however, that in the clearing pine-seedlings were already showing up. No doubt eventually they could replace the pine-trees that had been felled, thanks to this vandal's ignorance.

In a few years time I would have more success in finding a car-park in Tibet than cutting hazel-shanks in that piece of woodland.

Offcuts 2 - Stick Dressing

I am quite content myself to consider our craft as stick-making. This however is not good enough for some, they prefer to regard themselves as stick-*dressers*. There are even several associations catering for them. What an emotive word is "dress" in this context, conjuring up visions of intricately-carved and -coloured horn marvels, resplendent in their ranks at the shows. The creators of such beauties must surely be endowed with artistic abilities and other creative skills denied us less fortunate horny-handed labouring-classes. Naturally they need to be classified differently, you may think.

And how do such unskilled peasants as ourselves aspire to the ranks of the elite? Don't bother, it's all a myth. The facts are that if you trim a few side shoots on a shank, or do a little straightening you have started "dressing" it. There is no mystique about stick-dressing. It is none other than what we all do when we work on a shank; stick-*making*, in fact.

Offcuts 3 - If the Cap Fits...

Extract from a magazine-article by the secretary of a stick-making association - "A well-proportioned head is a thing of symmetrical beauty, and I find on looking around the various shows that a lot of sticks are not proportionate. This I think is also the same with the human head. Some are far too big and fewer are too small. Some have certain outstanding characteristics; big ears; too wide between the eyes - or too narrow; enormous teeth; mouths like letter-boxes ... and the same principles apply to the head of a crook."

I would imagine that association-members and fellow officials would be paying close scrutiny to their shaving mirrors following publication of this article.

Offcuts 4 - The Antler Retriever

The stalker on Speyside, from whom I get my antler, told me that his Labrador dog helped him tremendously when he was on the hill in springtime collecting cast-antler. The dog picked up (mainly in heather, where it is not always easy to see) nearly as many antlers as his son and himself did. It had become so proficient that it commonly carried two antlers at a time; and he gave a demonstration to show its prowess. He threw an antler about twentyfive feet away into rough grass, then another several yards away and told the dog to fetch. It had the first antler gripped by the middle in no time at all and made to bring it back until told to seek the other also. It ran across to the other, dropped the first one on top and in line with it, then after a few seconds nuzzling into position, had them both by the middle and returned. I was assured that there was little danger to the dog's eyes as his grip was too firm to prevent snagging.

Offcuts 5 - Extending Horns

Most tup-horns are fairly closely coiled. Many too, will have a hole drilled through near the tip. These are coupling-holes, whereby two tups are linked side-by-side, usually in the autumn, to prevent fighting. Horns are now often seen that are coiled out much further in an impressive spiral. These always have a hole, but this is because of a cosmetic "improvement" to their looks.

A piece of studding (threaded rod) is fixed across the horns and through the holes when the tup is young. The horns, whilst growing, are gradually trained further apart by adjusting nuts on the rods. These 'big horn' tups (an illusion - the horn is not any longer) are much in demand at the marts and always fetch higher prices I understand. One would have thought that a hard-headed farming community would not be so easily impressed (or fooled) and would pay more attention to the nuts at the other end of the tup.

Offcuts 6 - Instant Whistle-Stick

I'm often asked to make an antler-handle whistle-stick. Now I've never felt the need for a whistle myself as I was born with a perfectly good inbuilt one. This always gets my dogs' attention but if it's cold and my lips are like dried-prunes, a well directed "CUM ERE YE LITTLE BUGGERS!" works just as well.

Many stickmakers however, like to produce them, but this is not always easy; incipient hernias have frequently been induced by trying desperately to make the damn things whistle. I know of one who was determined to succeed. But could he get his efforts to whistle! He went through more antler-tips than the Monarch of the Glen would grow annually, and still not a peep.

Finally he said, "Sod it!", and went out and bought a child's plastic whistle, extracted the whistle part, inserted that into the antler-tip and - an instant whistle! You certainly need patience and ingenuity as a craftsman; not to mention a bit of low animal-cunning.

Offcuts 7 - Bending Breakthrough

The biggest problem encountered in horn-work is the heating and subsequent shaping. If you utilise my idea (evolved after years of experimentation) your troubles are over. I've used it on buffalo-horn, cow-horn, billy-goat- and tup-horn, all with first-class results. It even works with deer-antler, from which you can now make market-sticks and crooks.

You will need this special mixture (more about that later) which you put in your broth-pot and slowly bring up to the boil. Then simmer after putting in the horn. It doesn't matter if all of the horn is not submerged as the heat will travel. Keep an eye on the time, too, because even the bulkiest buffalo-horn requires only fifteen minutes. But, you must keep stirring, keep stirring, keep stirring,. KEEP STIRRING!!! ... "Arrgh!!!" - the Gaffer has elbowed me in the ribs and woken me up - "I know you love stirring things up, but do you have to keep saying it in your sleep?"

I've tried ever since to remember what I put in that mixture, but I'm buggered if I can!

Offcuts 8 - Stickmaking Secrets

The sayings of Confucius, the ancient Chinese philosopher, can have relevance even to stickmaking. This one in particular often applies: "The Master must teach the pupil everything - except how to become the Master."

Many experts tend to be squirrelly types, hoarding their little nuggets of knowledge like nuts or acorns. One prominent local stickmaker, being interviewed by the Press, stated that he "did not mind telling anyone anything" about the craft but would never divulge "how he straightened shanks." Another tutored at evening-classes on stickmaking under the auspices of the local Education Authority one autumn. But he did not continue after the New Year; the reason being, and I quote, "... the buggers only want to pick my brains!"

Offcuts 9 - Is It Horns You're After Wanting, Then?

An Irish stickmaking friend fancied having a go at horn-handles. So, like most of us have done, he spread the word around amongst friends and acquaintances - "any tup-horn?" Then he got a message that made his day - a bag of them were on the way. A large and heavy plastic fertiliser bag arrived a few days later and his heart leaped - until he emptied it. Out tumbled a fermenting mess of four rams' heads, complete with horns;

smelling bad enough to curl your hair, and lifting with larvae, maggots and bluebottles.

Offcuts 10 - Ask A Silly Question

The newcomer to the craft asks the Old Hand - "When's the best time to cut shanks?" - "There's *two* best times, lad. The first one's between Christmas and New Year," he was told. "That's handy, then, just when I'm off work. When's the other best time, then?" - "Between New Year and Christmas"!

Offcuts 11 - Ovine and Orotund

Reading a report of the Royal Welsh Show I was intrigued to see sheep classes for such exotically named breeds as Ile de France, Barrichon du Cher, Rouge de l'Quest, Vendeen, and Bleu du Maine. Now there's some real gobfulls there alright, and I mean the names, not the meat. I would have thought that with sixtyfive distinct breeds or types of sheep already in Britain, we could have got along nicely without more. And when you have Welsh breeds for instance with names such as Beulah Speckled Face, Kerry Hill, and Badger Faced, who needs continental varieties named like holiday resorts?

Mind you, I'd love to hear the auctioneer at the mart flogging some of these new ones; he'd be spluttering so hard that the first three rows would be wishing they were wearing their Barbour jackets.

As a matter of stickmaking interest, if they are not polled varieties, I wonder what their tup-horn is like - striped like a matelot's shirt, perhaps?

Offcuts 12 - Somewhere Just Off The A.1

I had ordered some tup-horn from a lad in the Midlands. Not something I'd do as a rule, as tup-horn, sight-unseen, can turn out a right pig-in-a-poke, but I have had horn from him previously, and could rely upon him. He said he would sort out what I required, and post it off. Then he rang a day or two later to say that it was on its way, as he had a friend coming up North who would drop it off "in my area", and I could pick it up. He couldn't remember where it was being delivered to, but was sure the place began with "H". It was certainly in the North East and he fancied it was Hartlepool (this is 50 miles from where I live!) - or it might have been Harrogate? (nearer 75 miles). Actually he thought that it was Harrogate, but I said that Harrogate was near Leeds and in Yorkshire, not exactly the North East. He then seemed a bit doubtful, but still sure it began with "H". So I suggested Halifax; Huddersfield; Holmfirth? - No, none of those. Could I think of anywhere else with "H" in the North East? How about Hebburn; Hexham; Haltwhistle; Haydon

Bridge? - No. Then he said to wait a minute or two and he'd look the address up and ring back. - It turned out to be Darlington! (40 miles away).

I'll bet geography was not his strong point at school, and he probably struggled a bit with the alphabet, too.

Offcuts 13 - The Joys of Stickmaking

I staggered home at dusk, across the fields and up the hill, one late afternoon in November. It had rained most of the day and I had suffered a strength-sapping, clothes-snagging and skin-tearing three hours. I was fit to drop, with fingers freezing, arms throbbing and rain down my neck. My boots were mud up to the ankles and trousers split from backside to belt. My thornproof jacket had turned out not to be, and I was cold, shivering, and puffing like an old cuddy. You could fairly say that I was knackered.

Mind you, I *did* have six holly-shanks and a brace of blackthorn for my efforts...

May all your shanks be well balanced and straight;
May deer cast their antler where you can always find them;
May your tup horn be large and solid;
And may the wind be always at your back -
Particularly if you are heating billy-goat horn.